OUTHOUSES *of* ALASKA

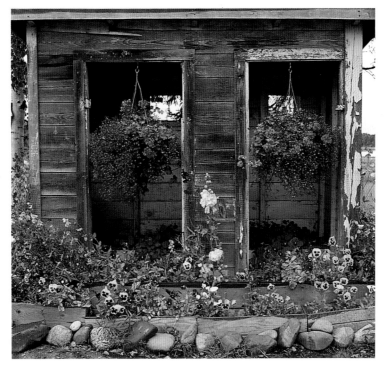

PHOTOGRAPHY AND STORIES BY HARRY M. WALKER

To Sylvia Bergel . . . Thanks.

Library of Congress Control Number: 2012902321
ISBN: 978-0-9819258-2-0 paperback

Published by Another Alaskan DoDad

Text Editor: Christine Ummel
Cover and Book Design: Elizabeth Watson
Proofreader: Lois Kelly
Printer: C & C Offset Printing Co., Ltd.
Production Coordinator: Susan Dupère

Distributed by Aftershocks Media

First edition hardbound, 1996
First edition softbound, 2012

10 9 8 7 6 5 4 3 2 1

Printed in China

To order single copies of OUTHOUSES OF ALASKA, mail $14.95 each plus $5.25 for shipping to:
Another Alaskan DoDad
6828 Cape Lisburne, Anchorage, AK 99504 or
go to www.anotheralaskandodad.com to order online.

Booksellers: This book is available from major wholesalers. Retail discounts are available. Contact Aftershocks Media at info@aftershocksmedia.com

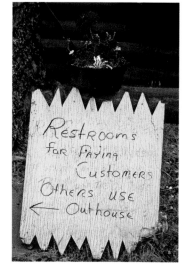

▶ A sign outside the Chistochina Lodge, on the Tok Cutoff Highway, offers explicit instructions to visitors.

FOREWORD

High time someone enshrined the outhouse in Alaska's archives! Perhaps no institution has contributed more to our democratization and development than this humble structure. ◗ Caring nothing for the creed, color, or social status of those who'd seek solace within its portals, one moment it accommodates the gnarled nates of a trail-toughened bush rat; the next, with equal magnanimity, the billowing buttocks of one to the manor born. ◗ What other institution would accept without complaint the indignities to which the outhouse is subjected? The legislature? The courts? The National Organization of Women? Forget it. By contrast, the outhouse invites abuse, forever turning the other cheek, so to speak. No one is denied access (save during prior occupancy) and never does an outhouse seek revenge upon even its most rank defilers . . . well, hardly ever. ◗ My Gramma Susie told of when she as a small girl took her pet piglet into a two-hole biffy, only to have it dive through the adjacent orifice. Even then there was a happy ending — for the pig. Gramma said little of the heroic efforts required to save the swimming swinelet, but pronounced he was retrieved and lived out his full life span. Seems few aspired to dine on sewage-marinated pork. ◗ The outhouse has at times accorded me refuge for reflection, snow shelter, immense relief, . . . and profound frustration. Like the time I accidentally locked myself in one and was reduced to shamefully hollering for help. (Tunneling to freedom seemed even less attractive. Besides, I had more than enough of that while yet in public office.) ◗ There's much more I could say about outhouses, but if you've ever used one you've probably already said it — perhaps in the howl of anguish elicited by the mortification of 98.6-degree flesh abutting minus 50-degree plywood? Or possibly an appropriate expletive torn loose upon the realization that the Sears Roebuck catalog had been stripped of all but its slickest pages? ◗ Of course, like most other institutions, with time's passage even the outhouse has not escaped character-corroding modifications. These make visitations of yesteryear seem all the more heroic: Styrofoam seat covers now often insulate one's nether-parts, and a more parsimonious Sears no longer supplies free toilet tissue. Instead, most biffies come equipped with rolls of T.P., often in effete pastels. ◗ Any wonder we today have no more heroes?

JAY HAMMOND
Former Governor of Alaska

CONTENTS

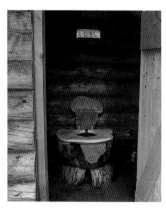

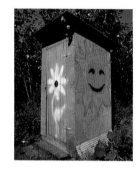

8 To complete this outhouse, master builder Harold Eastwood carved a throne out of one of nature's rarities.

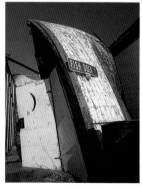

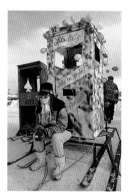

14 Homer Boat Yard owner Ben Mitchell found a new use for an old boat hull.

36 One Saturday each February, custom-made outhouses on skis are raced in Anchorage.

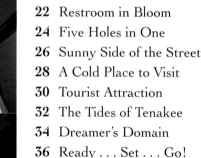

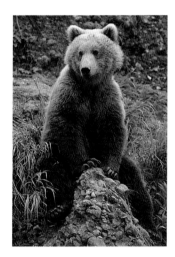

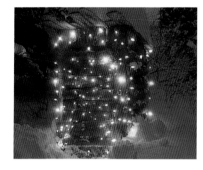

58 A string of Christmas lights made Claire Steffen's outhouse something to sing about.

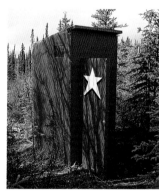

44 Outhouses always made Karen Moneymaker nervous, but she never expected to share one with a bear.

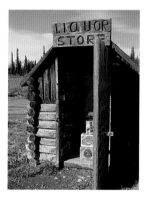

50 Visitors to Vernice Adkins' campground buy their booze at the "World's Most Unique Liquor Store."

63 The strange saga of a disappearing outhouse with a fireworks-style paint job.

INTRODUCTION

Get past all the bad one-liners about outhouses, and many people admit to strong feelings of nostalgia on the subject. Whether or not they have ever seen an outhouse or used one, people see the outhouse as a reminder of the "good old days." And though most of us have no idea exactly what that means, we would likely agree that the "good old days" had more of something the modern world lacks: privacy. We also would likely admit that our society has suffered as a consequence of that loss ☽ Outhouses were designed, either consciously or unconsciously, to provide privacy. They were quiet, earthy, dimly lit places, located away from the main house. An outhouse was a place for personal time, for contemplation or reading. If the outhouse happened to have a great view, all the better.

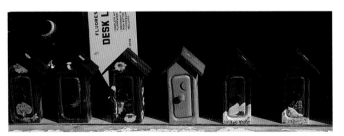

A visit to the outhouse was not an experience to be rushed, not even in mid-winter. Good reading material was as essential as toilet paper. Of course, in many cases, reading material *was* toilet paper . . . but the fact remains that the outhouse was a place to reflect, to muse, to ponder. Think about it. If outhouses were never intended for long, restful visits, why were they designed with seats? ☽ The modern bathroom is no substitute. There are precious few mental health benefits to be derived from a visit to a bathroom. A bathroom is serious business. It's a perfect example of cold, unemotional technology, full of porcelain, chrome, stainless steel, ceramic tiles, and bright lights. Centrally located in the house, the modern bathroom is often shared by several members of the family, especially at peak hours in the morning or evening. It has become increasingly common to have telephones installed or to keep a handy cordless phone nearby, so that you are never out of touch. Privacy in a modern bathroom is an illusion. ☽ Sadly, most of the United States, the modern bathroom has completely replaced the outhouse. Only in Alaska has the outhouse prevailed. In a place that revels in the fact that it

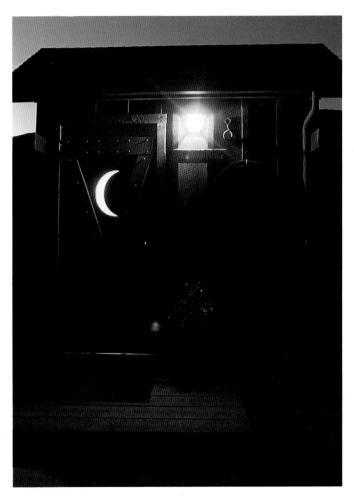

is different from anywhere else, the outhouse is a prime example of that "differentness." The outhouse has become a cultural icon in Alaska. Tiny wooden outhouses are carved, painted, and sold to tourists as souvenirs in summer. Specially built outhouses on skis

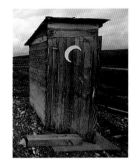

are raced on an icy track in Anchorage in winter. ☽ Many of the Alaska outhouses I photographed for this book reflect a conscious effort to make the outhouse experience different from the typical bathroom experience. For some Alaskans, that meant putting a little fun and lightheartedness into the experience, with outrageous decorations or collections of knickknacks and bric-a-brac. For others, it meant a return to the "good old days" in an outhouse with exceptional privacy, a restful decor, or the perfect reading environment. For still others, it meant locating the outhouse in a place with an inspiring view. Regardless, these outhouses embrace the notion that time spent within is time well spent.

◄ ◄ Miniature outhouses for sale at the hardware store in Skagway.
◄ The North Face Lodge outhouse in Kantishna, inside Denali National Park.
▲ The Dixon Creek Mine outhouse, on the Seward Peninsula.

MASTERPIECE

Harold and Vi Eastwood have homesteaded along the Nenana River near Denali National Park since 1967. One day, Harold, a master log builder for the National Park Service for nine years, found the perfect spruce burl on an old white spruce tree overlooking the river. Two feet across and nearly round, the burl would make the perfect log sink. Harold filed the location of the tree away in his head and waited for the opportunity to make use of his discovery. ☾ In 1973, Harold decided to build a rental cabin on

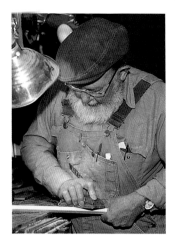

▲ At home in his workshop, master craftsman Harold Eastwood smoothes the surface of a wood detail for a neighbor's front door.
▶ Harold Eastwood built this spruce log outhouse on property near his homestead.

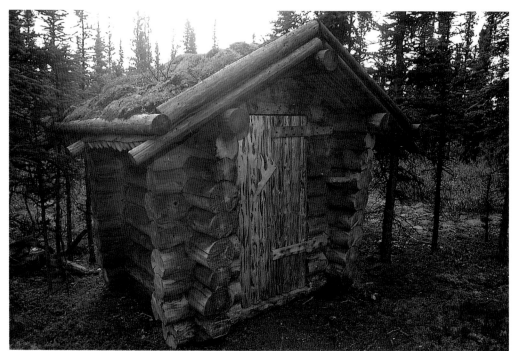

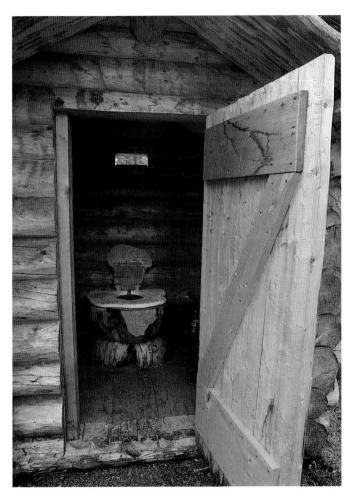

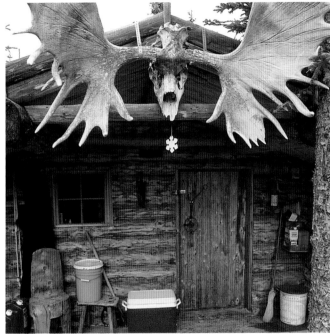

property he owned nearby. When it came time to build the outhouse (out of spruce logs, of course), Harold thought about that perfect burl. . . . The next thing he knew, that perfect burl sink became the perfect burl throne.

◄ The majestic-looking throne was carved out of a huge spruce burl, a round, tumor-like growth that forms on spruce trees.

▲ An enormous pair of moose antlers crowns the Eastwoods' rental cabin along the George Parks Highway.

A TOUCH OF CLASS

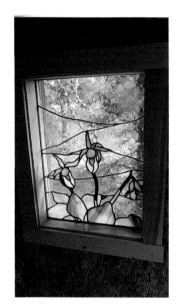

▲ Sunlight shines through a delicate stained glass window in Vi Eastwood's guest outhouse.
▶ Vi Eastwood relaxes in the kitchen of her home near Denali National Park.

After working for nineteen years at the Denali National Park Post Office, Vi Eastwood was looking for a new challenge. She was used to socializing with people in the tiny building near the Denali Park Hotel. Sitting home while her husband Harold pursued his second career making racing sleds for Iditarod mushers was not going to satisfy her. Vi decided to turn her homestead along the George Parks Highway into a bed-and-breakfast, so she persuaded Harold to build her a couple of cabins and an outhouse for guests. To provide an adequate amount of light while still maintaining an appropriate

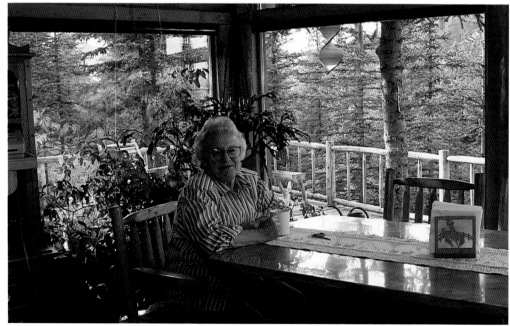

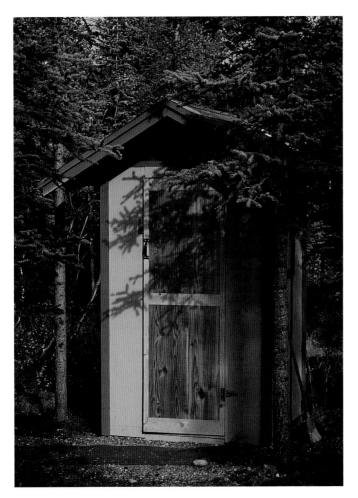

level of privacy, she commissioned local artist Pat Lee to create a stained glass window for the outhouse. "That stained glass made it special," Vi said.

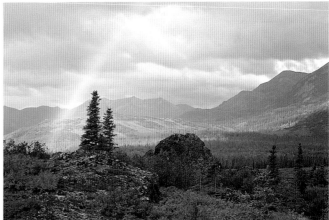

◀ Guests at the Eastwood Bed-and-Breakfast visited this elegant outhouse.
▲ Just down the road from the Eastwood homestead, a rainbow arches over the mountains of the Alaska Range.

A ROOM WITH A VIEW

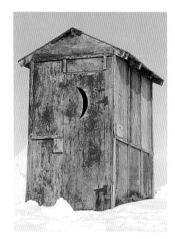

▲ This simple outhouse was built by famed Alaska pilot Don Sheldon.
▶ The towering, perpetually snow-covered peaks of the Alaska Range loom over the Sheldon outhouse.
▶▶ As seen from the outhouse, the summit of Mt. McKinley rises behind the West Fork of Ruth Glacier.

For an incredible view, few outhouses compare with this little wooden structure. It sits on an outcrop of rock at the 5,700-foot level of Ruth Glacier, which flows down the flank of Mt. McKinley, the tallest mountain in North America. Surrounded by some of the highest peaks in the Alaska Range, the outhouse is in the middle of an immense open area known as the Sheldon Amphitheater. The outhouse and nearby hut were built by legendary bush pilot Don Sheldon, who flew hundreds of mountaineers, skiers, and tourists onto the glacier for more than twenty years.

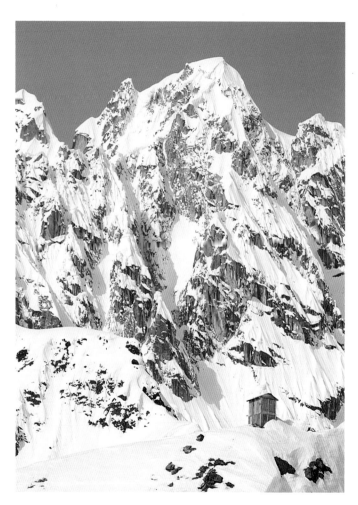

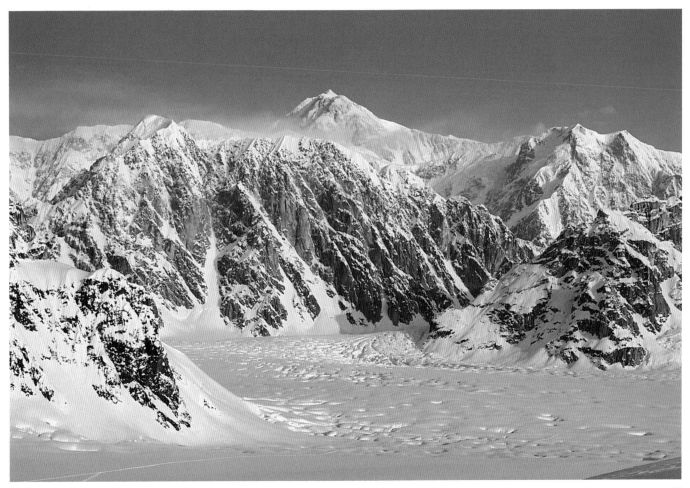

MARITIME METAMORPHOSIS

The old wooden boat hull sat in the back of the Homer Boat Yard when Ben Mitchell bought the place in 1980. "It was in the way," said Ben. "I had to do something with it." Did Ben hack it up for firewood, haul it off to the dump, or burn it where it lay? Nope! Ben was a believer in the old adage that when life hands you lemons, you should make lemonade. He took that old hull, cut it in half, stood it on end, put a door on it, dug a hole underneath it, and made it into the family outhouse. Ben told me he and his family used it full-time until he got indoor plumbing in 1985. "For a while all my customers took pictures of it," he said, seemingly surprised at the attention, "but after 1985 the outhouse was kind of forgotten. Now it's stuck behind all kinds of junk, but it's still there and it still works."

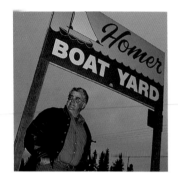

▲ Ben Mitchell, owner of the Homer Boat Yard.
▶ At twilight, the Homer Spit stretches into the waters of Kachemak Bay, with the Kenai Mountains in the background.
▶ ▶ Ben Mitchell turned this old boat hull into his family's outhouse.
▶ ▶ ▶ Daylight shines through the old planks of the wooden boat-turned-outhouse.

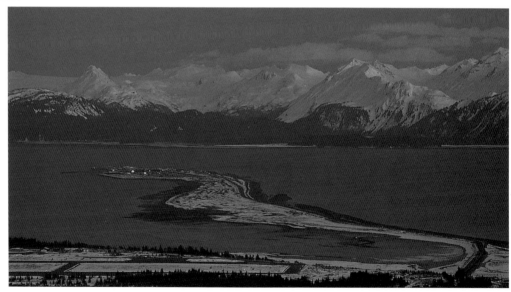

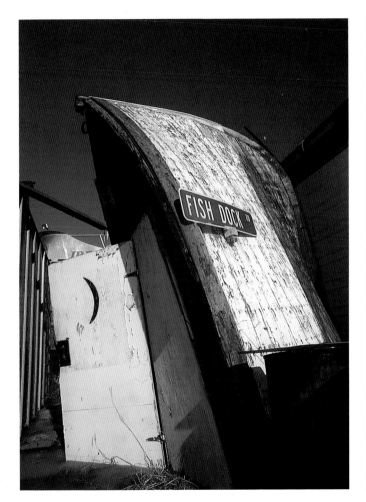

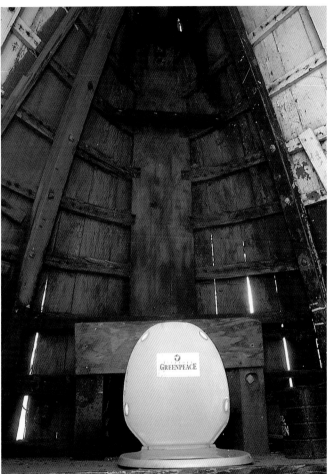

TAYLOR-MADE OUTHOUSE

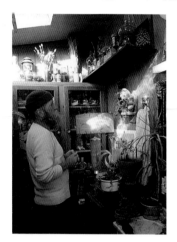

▲ Michael Taylor describes some of the items on display in his "museum" outhouse.
▶ An antique radio, a 1946 Las Vegas slot machine, and a gilded mirror are only a few of his countless treasures.

Michael Taylor has been collecting for a long time and takes his collecting seriously. A quick look around his seventeen acres near Fairbanks can tell you that. But the pièce de résistance of his work, the focal point of his talent, is his outhouse. Built in 1990 with help from his partner, a couple of friends, and scrounged materials (of course), the outhouse has an attached chicken coop, an arctic entry, men's and women's toilets, two skylights, a washbasin rigged with a forty-gallon plastic drum of water, and a front room large enough to hold a collection of . . . well, stuff. In fact, Michael Taylor's outhouse is nearly

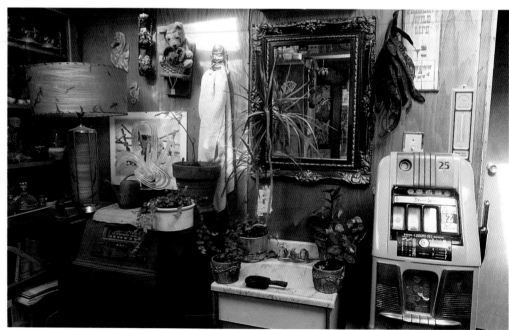

as big as the trailer he lives in. ☾ After looking at a few of his old vehicles, his man-made duck pond, and a couple of newly constructed buildings, we walked across the yard to begin a tour of his outhouse. Michael turned to me, a serious look on his face. "I want you to know, we didn't buy anything in here but two toilet seats. Even had those, but my partner didn't know and bought two on sale in town for $20." ☾ With that the tour of the outhouse began. Michael showed off his 1946 Las Vegas slot machine, an old console radio with no name but a look that dated back to the 1930s, display cases full of knick-knacks, glass figurines, beer cans, oil lamps, ceramic cups, shelves full of books, assorted plants everywhere, gilded mirrors, a bamboo chair, a 1983 hanging calendar with a picture of four multicolored parrots, an Einstein poster, and a live bird in a cage. Every piece of his collection came with a little story. He said that he could remember where everything in there had come from. I believe him. ☾ Michael hopes someday to build custom-made outhouses around Fairbanks. "I want to prove that you can live with an outhouse and have it be a pleasant experience," he said. No word whether these outhouses will come complete with their own mini-museums. If they do, I have no doubt about Michael's ability to fill them.

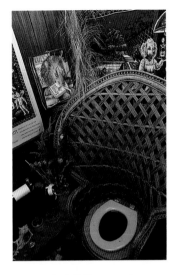

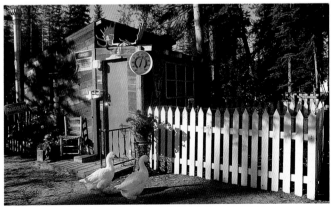

◄ A bamboo chair functions as one of two thrones in Michael Taylor's eclectic outhouse.
▼ Two geese wander by the fenced front yard of the outhouse, which is off Rosie Creek Road near Fairbanks.

LUNAR LEGACY

Ever wonder why outhouses are decorated with a crescent moon? The outhouse as we know it originated in Europe more than 500 years ago. In the fifteenth and sixteenth centuries, Europe experienced an amazing burst of economic growth and prosperity. Trade boomed as an expanding network of roads brought the towns, cities, and countries of Europe closer together. Roadside inns were built throughout Europe to serve the needs of the ever-increasing numbers of tourists and traveling salesmen. To attract customers, the finer inns began offering "his" and

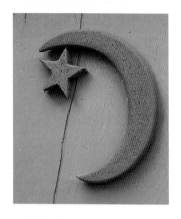

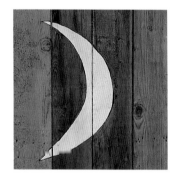

A collage of crescent moon designs from all over Alaska:
▲ Tent City, Skagway.
▶ The McNamara home, Sutton.
▶▲ The Rhoads home, Soldotna.
▶▶ Glacier Bay Country Inn, Gustavus.
▶▶▶ The Kennecott Mines, Kennicott.

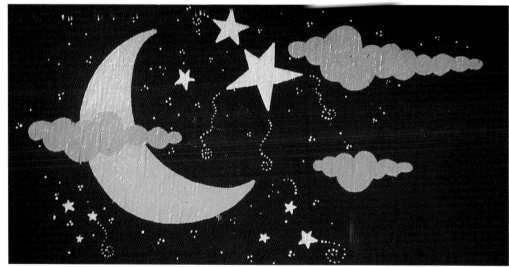

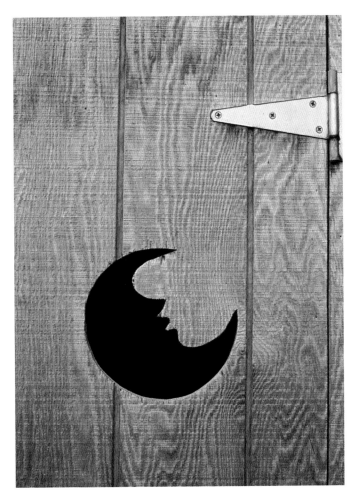

"her" outhouses. 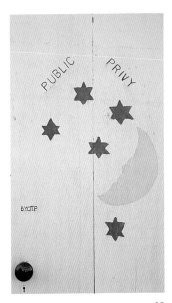 Because most people were illiterate, symbols were used on outhouses to show which was "his" and which was "hers." Pictures of the sun and the moon were the obvious choice. From ancient times, the sun had been a symbol of all that was masculine and the moon of all that was feminine. Outhouse doors across Europe were marked with either a sun or a crescent moon (a full moon would have been confusing). As time passed, inns and outhouses sprang up everywhere. Competition was intense, and innkeepers were always looking for ways to cut costs. Looking at the bottom line, innkeepers reasoned that maintaining a men's outhouse was unnecessary. Men could always find a spot in the woods—and those who couldn't or wouldn't use the woods would just use the women's outhouse. Men's outhouses disappeared, leaving only women's outhouses, marked with the crescent moon.

ALL PLUSHY
NO FLUSHY

Maggie and Dusty Rhoads (no kidding) moved their young family from Idaho to Alaska in 1982. Not long after, they found their dream property at the end of Rabbit Run Road, about eight miles from Soldotna near Brown's Lake. The first house they built was small and had no running water, so an outhouse was built along with it. "We used that outhouse for a long time before we built another house," Maggie recalled during a conversation we had at a picnic table in her yard. "We had it carpeted for ourselves. It is another room of our house, and we wanted it to be comfortable. You know it's got to be there. You've got

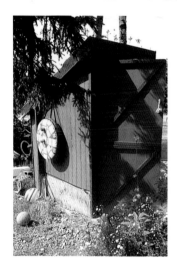

▲ Dutch doors give visitors to the Rhoads' outhouse a little privacy and a view of the great outdoors.
▶ Maggie Rhoads and her seven children share a "quiet" moment at their homestead near Soldotna.
▶ ▶ To make it cozy, the Rhoads family carpeted their outhouse from floor to ceiling.

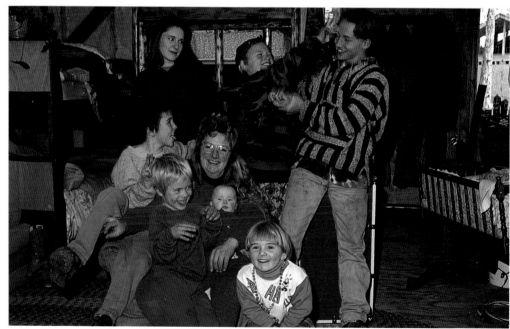

20

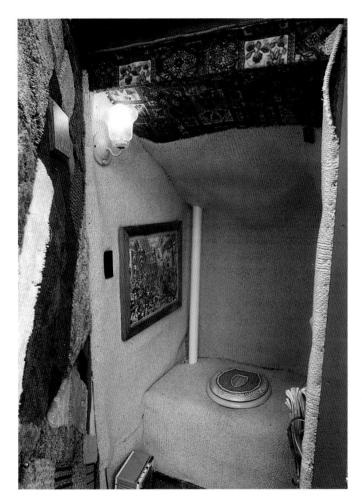

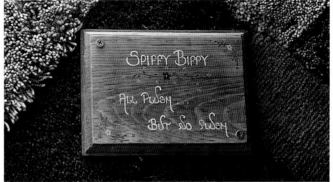

to have one until you have running water. We wanted it to be as nice as we could make it." 🌙 She looked over to the outhouse with a broad smile. "We really have enjoyed the Dutch doors, my husband especially. He still uses the outhouse. With seven kids, he enjoys it—it's private. He can open that top door and look at nature. He enjoys himself, and it's a lot better for the rest of us." 🌙 Pointing to a little plaque on the inside of the upper Dutch door, Maggie said, "A friend's mother thought the outhouse was the neatest thing she had ever seen: a carpeted outhouse! She gave me the little painting:

> *Spiffy Biffy*
> *All Plushy . . .*
> *But No Flushy."*

RESTROOM IN BLOOM

When Helen Tucker and Stella Hughton bought the Willow Trading Post, the old double outhouse next to the rental cabins hadn't been used for years. Helen believes that the outhouse dates to the 1940s, when the little cabins behind the bar and restaurant were built. Slowly the cabins were replaced with newer buildings that included private bathrooms. The outhouse was used less frequently. Eventually it just sat there, forgotten.

After Helen and Stella took over the place in 1981, Helen planted gardens all over the property, which, over the years, became a local attraction. Helen worked hard to keep them up until the trading post was sold in 1993. "I've been into gardening for over fifteen years," she said. "I enjoyed doing it, even though it was a lot of work. I started all of the flowers from seeds each year—started them in February and March, inside, of course. I replanted them outside the first week in June. It took me a couple of days to plant the ones around the outhouse: nasturtiums in the toilet seats and fuchsia in the hanging baskets. I changed the color theme every year." When I asked Helen where she got the idea of turning an outhouse into a planter, she answered, "Life is a toilet filled with flowers."

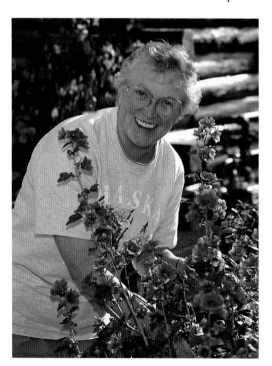

▶ Helen Tucker looks up from tending a bed of hollyhocks.
▶ ▶ Under her care, the old double outhouse became part of the Willow Trading Post's beautiful gardens.

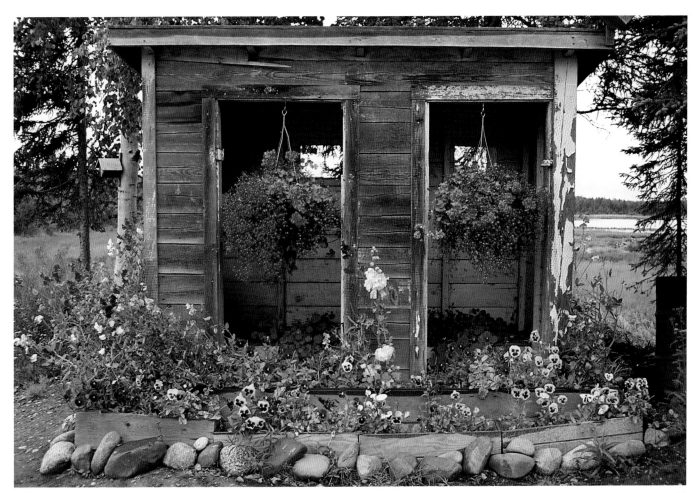

FIVE HOLES IN ONE

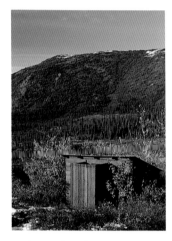

▲ The Wonder Lake Ranger Station men's outhouse, in the middle of Denali National Park, stands in front of the Kantishna Hills.
▶ Five seats, all in a row, await a sudden rush of park backpackers.
▶▶ Sunset over Mt. McKinley gives the sky an autumn glow.

The Wonder Lake Ranger Station is in the heart of Denali National Park, some eighty-six miles from the park entrance. Relatively few visitors make it this far down the park's main road. You wonder what might have been in the minds of the federal bureaucrats responsible for designing the ranger station's five-seater for men. Did they anticipate crowds of suffering male backpackers showing up at the ranger station all at once? I can picture a group of Federal Outhouse Engineers, sitting at desks lined one next to the other, running computer simulations to decide whether five seats would be enough. Do they really think guys are that social?

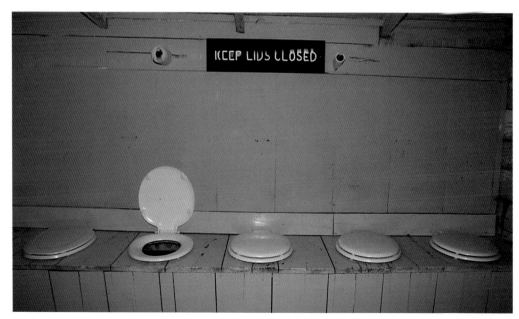

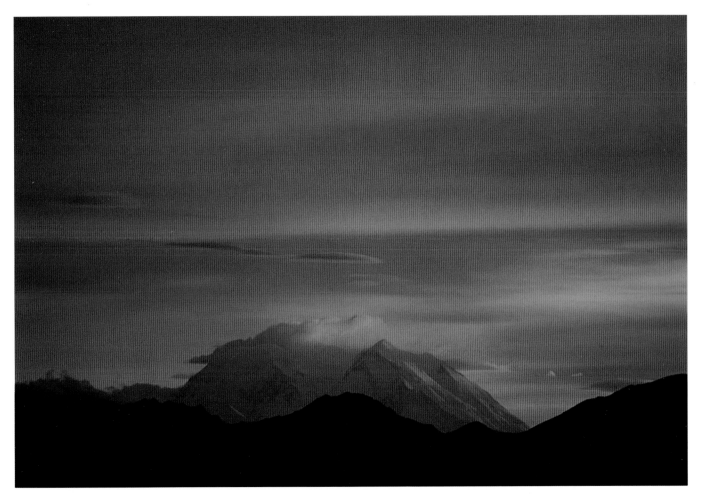

SUNNY SIDE OF THE STREET

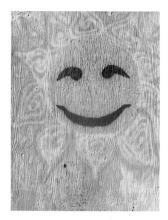

▲ A close-up of the sun painted on Meg Helmer's outhouse.
▶ Some of Eagle's turn-of-the-century buildings front the Yukon River.

Meg Helmer moved to Eagle, a small community of 175 people along the Yukon River, in the summer of 1987 when she married a local boy who had lived there nearly all his life. She was from an army family and had moved from post to post, house to house, as she grew up. She had lived in many places but nowhere quite like Eagle. ☽ Meg and her new husband moved downtown, into a small corner house with an unpainted outhouse out back. Of course, calling the corner of Amundsen and First "downtown" is a relative matter. The streets are dirt, there are no sidewalks, and the nearest commercial building is a couple of blocks away. But the house is only a few blocks from the Yukon River in one

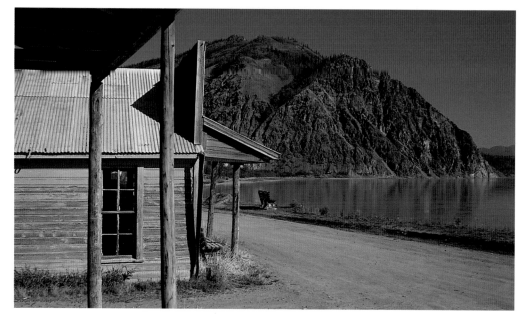

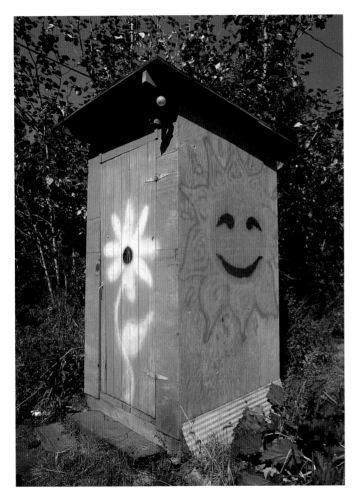

direction and a few yards from the town pump house in another. In a town with no central water system, the pump house is a center of activity. Nearly everyone passes by Meg's corner and her outhouse. ☽ All that first summer, people warned Meg that winters in Interior Alaska were long and dark. The key to making it through, her neighbors said, was a good attitude. One morning, with the dark months of winter approaching, Meg made a personal contribution to the positive attitude of the community. "I wanted to see the sun every morning, all winter," Meg told me. "I wanted everyone who came downtown to see the sun." Though Meg admits she is a little embarrassed now

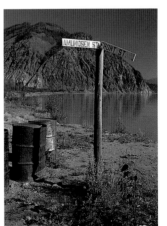

about painting the sun and flower on her outhouse eight years before, she also admits that it worked. "Regardless of the weather or the darkness, that sun was always there. It made me feel better."

◀ ◀ To bring a little sunshine to dark winter days, Meg Helmer gave a new paint job to her old outhouse.
◀ Signs mark two of the main streets in downtown Eagle.

A COLD PLACE TO VISIT

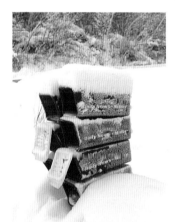

▲ Along Chena Hot Springs Road near Fairbanks, snow piles up on a stack of newspaper boxes.
▶ A path is worn through freshly fallen snow to an outhouse located near a cabin in the Chena River State Recreational Area.
▶ ▶ The winter sun sets early over the frozen Chena River.

Using an Alaska outhouse in winter is not without certain risks. Between cold, darkness, and wild animals, an outhouse visit can turn into an adventure. I heard a story about a young man who, after a trip to his outhouse, found he had accidentally locked himself out of his cabin at forty below, wearing nothing more than his long johns. Luckily he was able to get to his next-door neighbor's house before freezing to death. ☾ Alaska outhouses require a few special adaptations for winter use. You don't ever want to sit on a plastic or wooden toilet seat at twenty below. Consequently, some outhouse owners vary their seat covers from summer to winter. I have visited outhouses outfitted with cardboard (fairly slick and still a mite cold), Styrofoam (easily cracked), and carpeting (prone to causing rug burns). One owner I met took the matter more seriously. For years she made the effort to sew skin covers for her family outhouse seat, alternating from year to year between rabbit (comfortable but not durable) and beaver (the best).

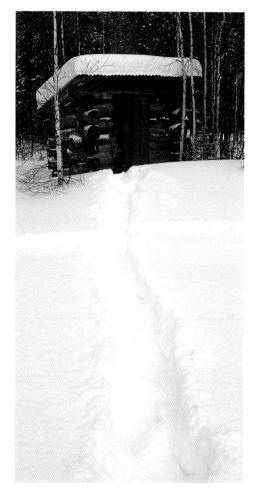

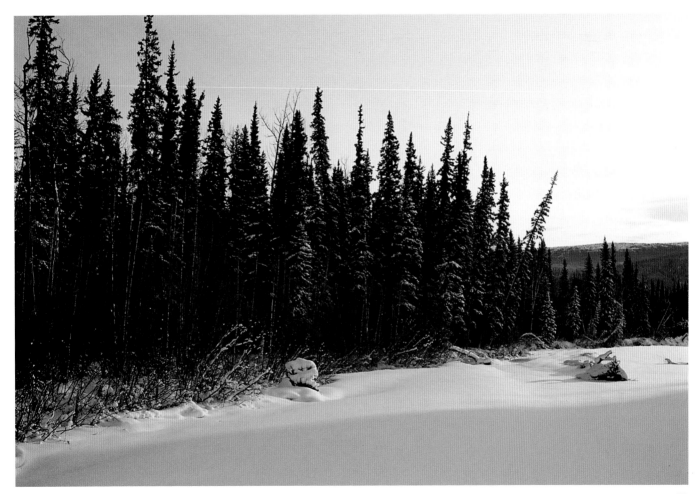

TOURIST ATTRACTION

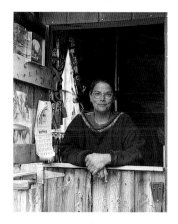

▲ Connie Bennett looks out the open top door of her McCarthy outhouse.
► The old town of McCarthy, set in the middle of Wrangell-St. Elias National Park, draws visitors from around the world.
► ▲ The cabin where Connie Bennett now lives was once used by a U.S. commissioner.
► ► One feature makes this outhouse unique — its urinal, made out of an old coal bucket.

Part ghost town, part living museum, McCarthy is a community trying to come to terms with its new-found popularity. Located in a beautiful area of mountains, glaciers, and rivers, it is a remnant of the heady days of the nearby Kennecott Mines, the world's largest copper mines until their closure in 1938. For most years since, McCarthy's population has been tiny. Then in 1980 Congress designated the 12 million acres around McCarthy the Wrangell-St. Elias National Park (the nation's largest), and life hasn't been the same since. An ever-increasing number of climbers, river runners, hikers, mountain bikers, tourists, and tourism developers have discovered the town. Locals are struggling with all the new attention. 🌙 Connie Bennett,

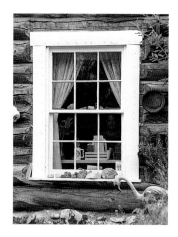

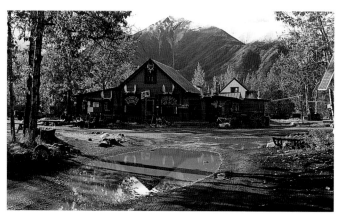

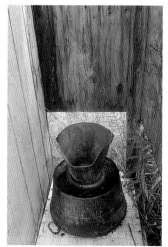

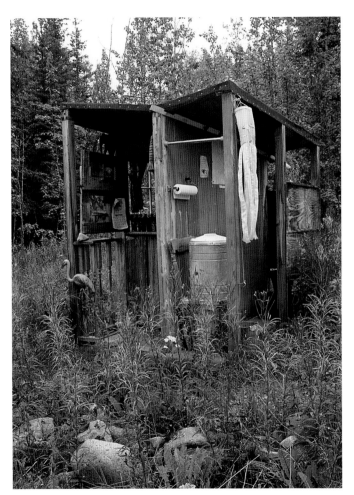

a former Anchorage resident and now a cook at the McCarthy Lodge, lives in an old two-story log cabin once used by a U.S. commissioner. But it isn't the historic cabin that summer visitors want to see—it's her outhouse. Connie has had to get used to the attention since her outhouse became a stop along the town's walking tour. When she moved in, Connie told me, she inherited an old outhouse built behind the cabin. In 1987, her friend Steve Cremer designed and constructed a new outhouse for her, using leftover lumber from around town. "Steve built it," Connie said, "because he was the only one around who could use a circular saw and keep all his fingers." Connie admits they got carried away when they dug the hole for the outhouse. "That hole was so big we didn't know what to do with it, so we used an old coal bucket and added a urinal." Connie went on to explain another feature of the outhouse that has made it a local favorite. The wind sock was intended to save people a long, unnecessary walk from the cabin. "It was supposed to let people know if the outhouse was occupied," Connie said. "But some people thought wind sock up meant occupied, others thought wind sock down. It got confusing."

◀ The outhouse, decorated with a wind sock and pink plastic flamingos, has become a regular stop on the McCarthy walking tour.

THE TIDES OF TENAKEE

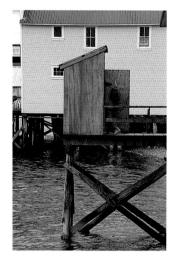

The tiny town of Tenakee Springs (population 95) is perched literally on the edge of Chichagof Island, some fifty miles northeast of Sitka. The town is squeezed so tightly between the beach and a steep, rocky slope that it has only one street, which runs from four to twelve feet wide. There is so little flat ground available that many buildings, including the general store, the fire station, and the post office, sit on stilts over the beach. Founded at the turn of the century, the town has no central water system or waste system. The people of Tenakee Springs resolved their waste disposal problem with a simple solution: the ocean givith, the ocean taketh away. More recently, modern technology has offered high-tech alternatives, but most residents continue to take the low-tech approach. When visitors arrive to sample the wonderful hot springs that gave Tenakee its name, town folk often provide a simple piece of advice: Be careful where you walk on the beach at low tide.

▲ A visitor to Tenakee Springs enters one of the town's many outhouses built on pilings over the water.
▶ On Chichagof Island in Southeast Alaska, much of the town of Tenakee extends out over the high tide line.
▶▶ Candlelight shines in the window of one of the town's more picturesque outhouses on a summer evening.

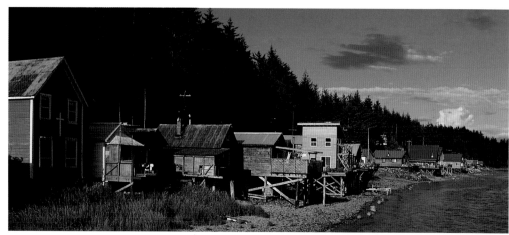

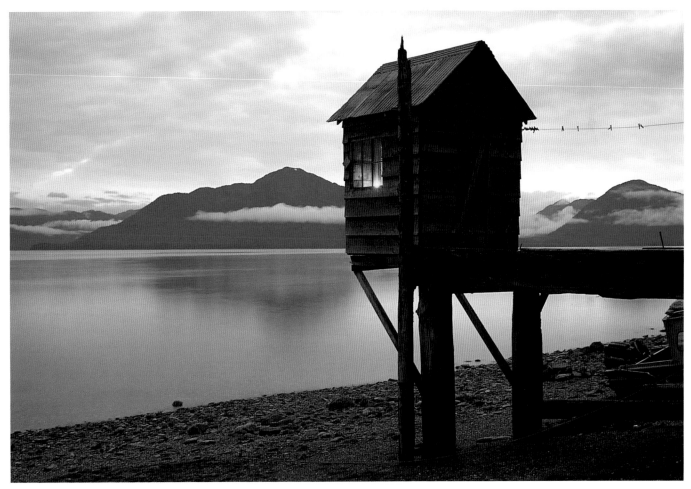

DREAMER'S DOMAIN

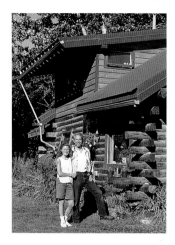

▲ Jerry and Carol McNamara, in front of their small log house near Sutton.
▶ Oak, polished brass, and a potted plant decorate this orderly outhouse.

Every August at the Alaska State Fair in Palmer, Jerry and Carol McNamara sell popcorn from a black walnut, glass, and antique brass wagon they built with their own hands. However, to call the McNamaras popcorn vendors is to seriously misrepresent them. Jerry is a dreamer and philosopher. He writes little kernels of wonderfully insightful observations on life and nature (his friends call it "popcorn philosophy") inside Carol's handmade cards or on the backs of unusual postcards, discovered in the dusty bins of antique shops. Carol is an artist, weaver, calligrapher, and lover of gardens and flowers. Their small log house on a ridge overlooking the Matanuska River valley is a remarkable

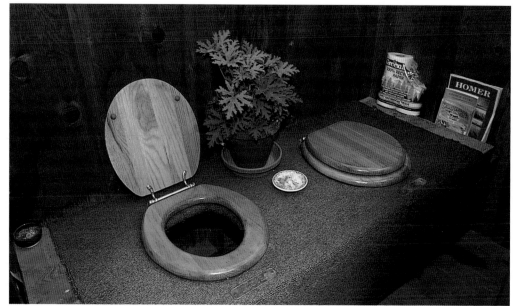

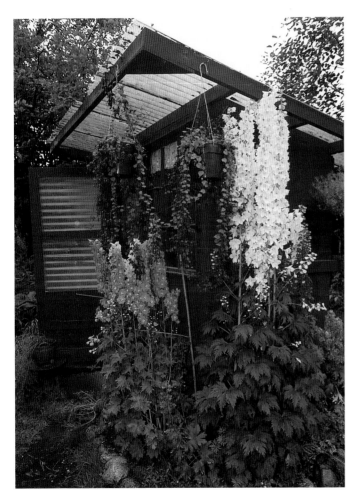

model of organized cabin living; a varied collection of antiques, art work, and memorabilia is efficiently arranged and always tidy. Their outhouse, set some fifty yards from the cabin, surrounded by lush beds of flowers in summer and neat banks of snow in winter, is a reflection of Carol's sense of order. Yet the outhouse is also a reflection of Jerry's philosophical nature. It's a great place to think. A visit to the McNamara outhouse is as restful and contemplative an experience as you could ask for.

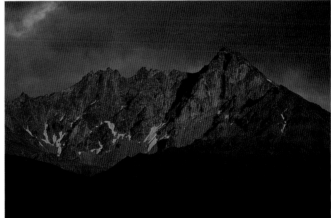

◄ Abundant flower beds surrounding the McNamara outhouse contribute to its quiet, restful atmosphere.
▲ The Chugach Mountains of the Matanuska River valley glow in the light of the setting sun.

35

READY...
SET...GO!

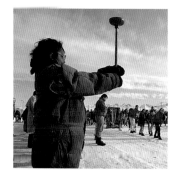

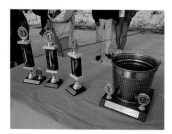

Highlights from the Outhouse Classic, part of the annual Anchorage Fur Rendezvous.

One Saturday every February, Anchorage residents race custom-built outhouses on skis across a frozen expanse of downtown parkland in an event known as the Outhouse Classic. From the ceremonial dropping of the plunger by Miss Latrina to the presentation of the coveted Golden Honey Bucket, the Outhouse Classic endeavors to raise the status of the Alaska outhouse from utilitarian necessity to cultural icon. ◗ Each outhouse-racing team consists of ten weirdly costumed individuals: four males and four females out front pulling, one person pushing from the rear, and one person sitting inside. Trophies are awarded not just to the swiftest outhouse but also to the most elaborate and the most bizarre.

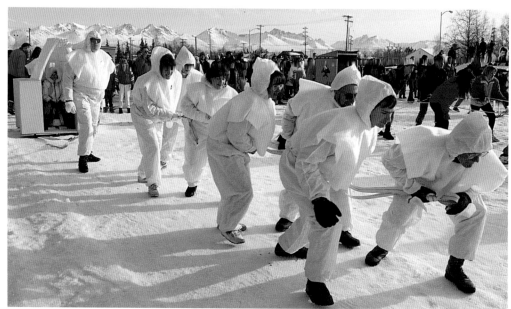

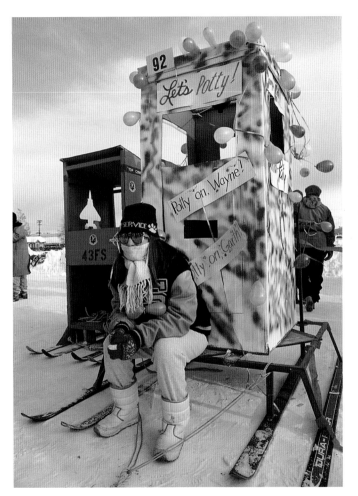

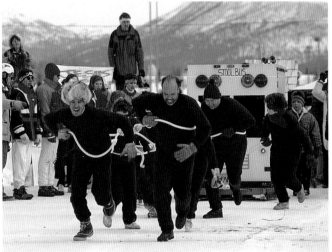

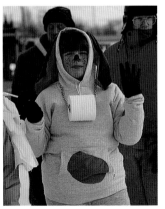

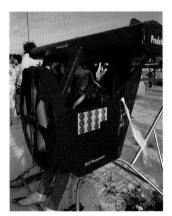

HIDEAWAY HAVEN

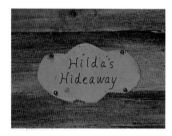

▲ A strip of moose hide honors this outhouse's most faithful visitor.
▶ Hilda Weishahn uses her son's outhouse, outside Haines, as her own private retreat.
▶ ▶ Drivers cruising south along the Haines Highway are treated to a spectacular view of Mt. McDonnell.

Hilda Weishahn lives in California. When she comes to Haines to visit her son Ron and his family, she loves to sit in the old outhouse out back, catch a smoke, and look out across the valley toward the Klehini River and the distant Jarvis Glacier. The outhouse reminds her of her childhood in North Dakota; it is a calm and restful place. It doesn't matter that there has been a bathroom in her son's house for many years. That outhouse is Hilda's place, so in 1981 Ron's family named the outhouse in her honor: "Hilda's Hideaway." And lest there be any doubt of ownership, they painted the name on a piece of moose hide and nailed it up for all to see.

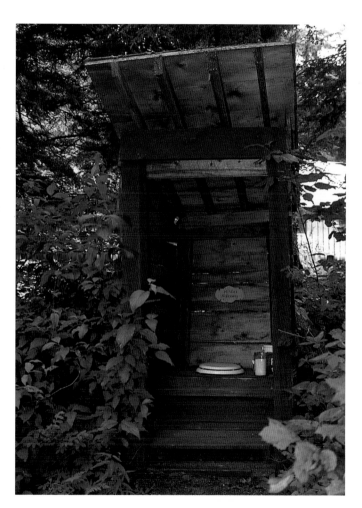

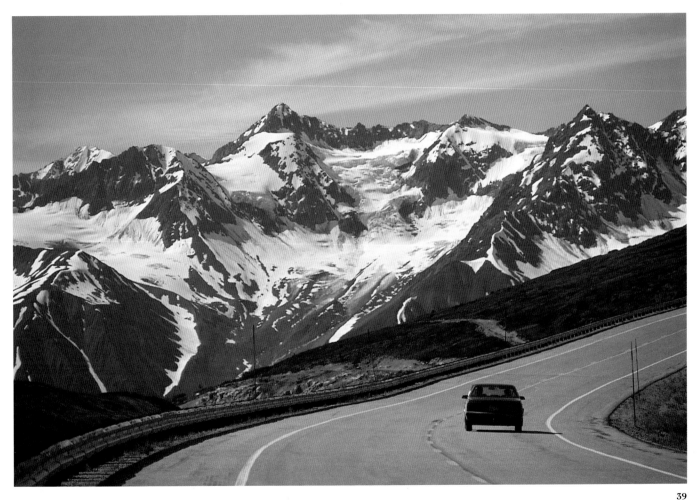

POLITICALLY INCORRECT

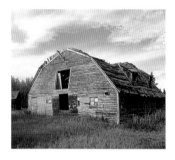

▲ A weathered barn in the town of Copper Center.
▶ One Copper Center resident used his outhouse to express his opinion of local politics.

Alaskans have a well-deserved reputation for political independence. More than one of every two Alaskan voters is registered nonpartisan or undeclared, the highest percentage of independent voters in the nation. Alaskans also have been known to express their opinions about politics in rather original ways. This sign, nailed on the side of an outhouse standing in a field in the small town of Copper Center (population 500), is a perfect example.

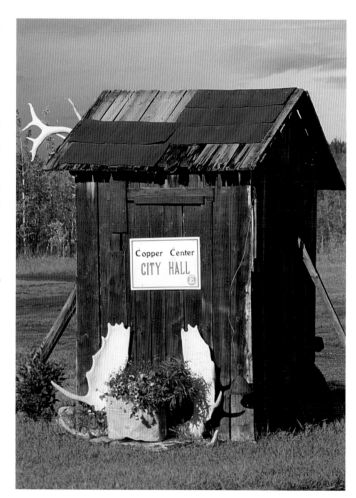

SOMETHING FISHY

In a place with thousands of miles of fish-rich rivers and streams, millions of lakes, and more miles of coastline than the rest of the country combined, fishing is serious business. Alaskans drink in bars named after salmon, use wallets made from salmon skin, and eat lots of salmon that has been dried, smoked, broiled, baked, fried, or poached. It's no surprise, then, that the folks at the Talkeetna Visitor Center got a little carried away with fishing references when it came time to put names on the "his" and "hers." For those of you who think "Chum" means buddy and "Dolly" is a Broadway musical, let me set you straight. Chums are a variety of salmon, the most widely distributed salmon in the Pacific. "Dolly" is short for Dolly Varden, a freshwater fish often called a trout but really a char.

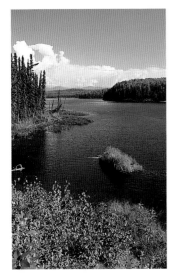

▲ Fish Lake, near the Talkeetna Visitors Center, serves as a floatplane base for Talkeetna as well as a popular fishing hole.

▶ In the heart of sportfishing territory, the Talkeetna Visitors Center offered fishing folk a set of restrooms they could relate to.

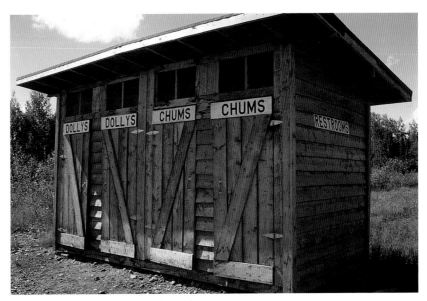

PRIZE-WINNING PRIVY

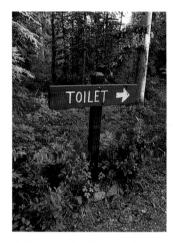

▲ An arrow points the way to Donna Bernhardt's outhouse.
▶ Donna Bernhardt's cat Siam sits in the doorway of this award-winning outhouse.
▶ ▶ Today the Governor's Choice Award hangs on the back wall of the Bernhardt outhouse.

In 1987 the *Cordova Times* sponsored its first annual outhouse contest, promising participants that their outhouses "would assume a coveted place in Alaska history." Twenty-three outhouses were nominated. The newspaper asked then-Governor Steve Cowper to pick the winner of the "Governor's Choice Award." According to the governor, it was a tough job, but after lengthy thought, he chose the outhouse of writer Donna Bernhardt of Tok. Wrote the governor: "I truly believe your own personal outhouse is an outstanding example of Alaska's unique, colorful, and well-used outhouses." ◗ According to Donna's *A History of One Great Alaskan Outhouse*, Donna, her husband Dick, and their two children moved to Tok from Anchorage in 1977. Though they started building their cabin as soon as possible, they were caught by an early winter and had to live in a tent for thirteen months. "An outhouse was not a high priority, at first," Donna recalled, "just a throne in a snowbank. We called it

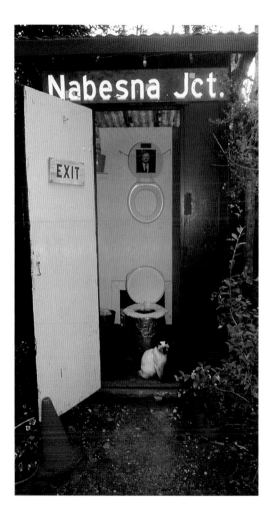

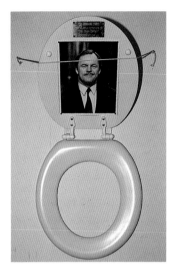

our 'out'. We didn't have a house around our 'out' for a couple of years." 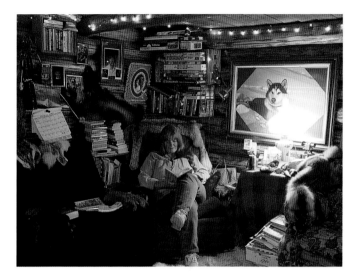 After a plane buzzed their "out" while Dick was using it, he and Donna decided a little effort was required to ensure their privacy. Using a couple of pieces of scrap plywood, Dick constructed a quick A-frame over their throne. It was far from perfect, but it did discourage curious pilots. That outhouse lasted about a year. The outhouse that won the contest was given to them by a state employee, who was going to trash the old outhouse from a nearby state campground. "I think he felt sorry for us," Donna told me. The Bernhardts hauled it home in the back of their truck and shoved it into place over the original throne. They added a few signs, some Christmas lights in winter, and voilà: an award-winning outhouse.

▶ ▲ On a summer evening, Donna Bernhardt relaxes with a good book in her log cabin home.

▶ The Bernhardts built their cabin from spruce logs and decorated it with snowshoes and caribou racks.

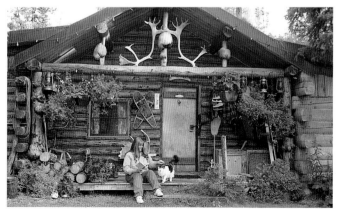

CLOSE ENCOUNTERS

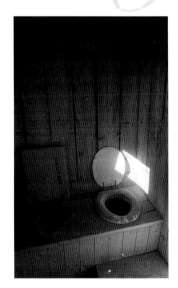

▲ A spot of sunlight falls into the shadows inside an abandoned outhouse on Chamberlain Avenue in Eagle.

▶ A mischievous young brown bear sits astride a rock at Mikfik Creek.

Just about everyone who uses an outhouse has an "encounter story." Tales abound about outhouse visitors meeting moose, bear, caribou, wolves, and all manner of wild creatures. ◗ One of the wildest encounters happened to Karen Moneymaker more than ten years ago, during a visit to her parents' cabin along the Salcha River, southeast of Fairbanks. While there, Karen had occasion to use the family outhouse. It was oddly quiet when she entered: no sound of bees or other insects buzzing, not even a peep from the resident squirrel. "I should have known something was up," she said. "It was so quiet. Too quiet." ◗ Apparently, a small grizzly had dug a hole under the back corner of the outhouse and had crawled down in search of some recently discarded bacon grease. Karen didn't know that—at least not yet. Karen admits that

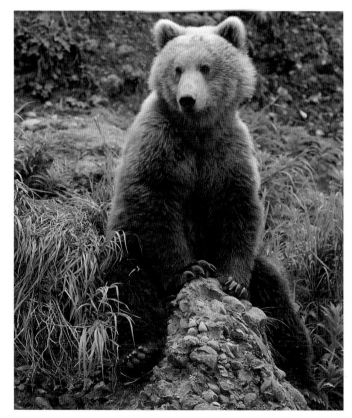

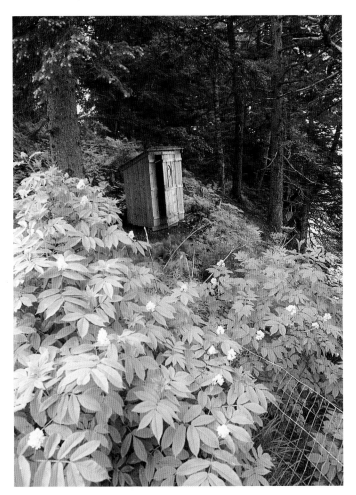

ever since she was a little kid she has been uncomfortable about outhouses. "When I used an outhouse, I always took a look down the hole. I felt so vulnerable. I was always worried about getting stung by a bee or something. Of course, I never expected a bear." 🌙 Just as Karen was taking her usual peek, the bear let out a grunt and Karen took off so scared she could hardly speak. The bear, probably as upset by the experience as Karen, beat a hasty retreat from the hole. 🌙 Now whenever Karen is confronted with a visit to an outhouse, she sends her husband in first to check it out. A poem written afterward by neighbor Tom Conley, entitled "Shoot-Out at the Shit-House," pretty much says it all:

> *She sat in the outhouse without a care*
> *Then a racket arose from the hole down there*
> *She did something you would never dare*
> *It happened she pissed on a grizzly bear.*

◀ Near Seldovia, an outhouse stands amidst lush vegetation at Lindar's Beach.

FOLK ART AMBIENCE

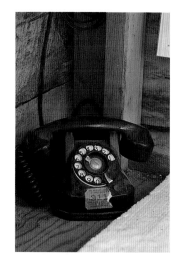

▲ This vintage telephone hasn't rung in years, but it has a home in Craig Buchanan's outhouse.

▶ Craig Buchanan considers his outhouse, in the old gold-rush town of Ester, to be a folk art sculpture in progress.

Craig Buchanan is a folk art sculptor with a lot to say about outhouses. "They represent personal freedoms . . . people decorate them a certain way, construct them a certain way, hide them a certain way, and expose them a certain way. There is a lot of inner perspective in outhouses."

When Craig bought his property in 1978, it came with several outhouses, all basically used up. After a few years of nursing the old outhouses along, he decided to build his own out of spruce wood and parts of all the other outhouses.

Craig regards the outhouse as a piece of folk art. "Like this ceramic cup," he explained, holding up a

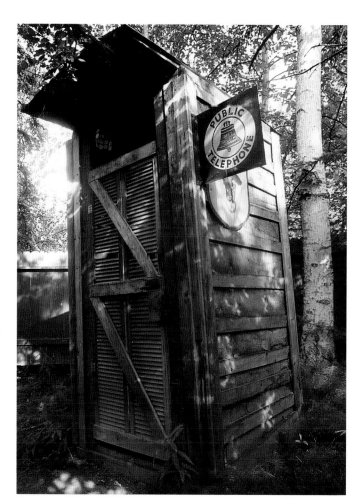

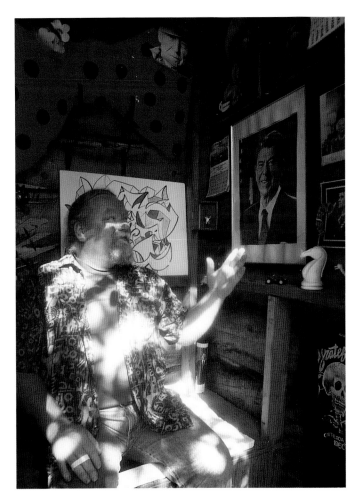

handmade coffee mug, "you can always take the piece and enjoy it in its utilitarian sense, but also you can look at it historically . . . somebody wanted to say something about something. Whether it was significant or not is pretty subjective, but you can always tell that somebody took time with this piece." ◗ For Craig, outhouses, like handmade cups, are one of the few utilitarian things still made in America that reflect the individuals who make them. "Bathrooms are generic and chrome and ninety-degree. Outhouses are more, I guess I would call them, ambient."

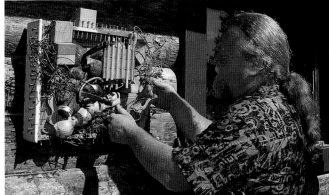

◀ Craig Buchanan points out favorite elements of his outhouse's interior, such as a giant bow tie and a framed photo of Ronald Reagan.
▲ As a folk artist, Craig Buchanan creates sculptures out of objects other people have discarded.

ON THE EDGE

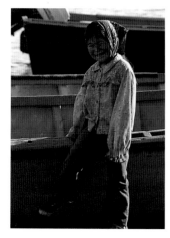

▲ A young Yupik Eskimo girl plays along the riverfront in the village of Pilot Station.
▶ On the bank of the lower Yukon River, this outhouse seems ready to collapse at any moment.
▶ ▶ After tying his boat to the shore, a lone canoeist sets off down the mudflats that line the lower Yukon River.

In 1975, while canoeing the Yukon River from its headwaters in British Columbia to the Bering Sea, I visited the small Yupik Eskimo village of Pilot Station. Most villages along the river had no central water or sewer systems, so outhouses were common. Many were set off in the woods or hidden among collections of outbuildings. This particular outhouse, however, sat precariously on the edge of the riverbank . . . *very much* on the edge of the riverbank. It was hard to tell whether it had been abandoned to the whim of the river. But after days of braving the woods with a roll of paper in one hand and a can of insect repellent in the other, any outhouse, even this one, was hard to resist.

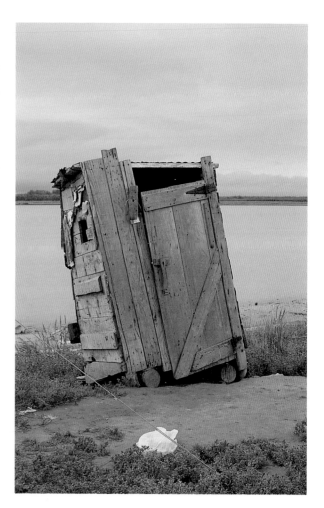

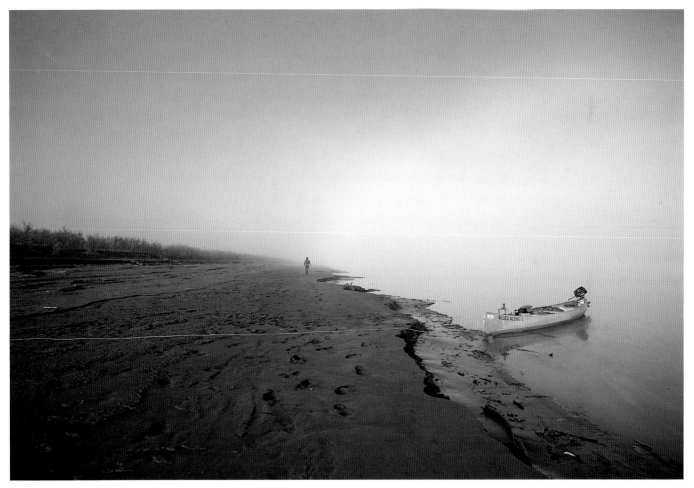

LIQUIDATION SALE

He calls it the "World's Most Unique Liquor Store." Who can argue? Twenty-four years ago, Vernice and Carol Adkins from Miami, Florida, decided to live out their dream. They bought a couple of old buildings, built back in the 1940s, with a campground attached alongside the Little Mendeltna River. Shortly after taking over the place, Vernice replaced the old Kamping Resorts of Alaska two-seater outhouse with modern facilities. What did he do with the outhouse? He tore out the seats and made it a

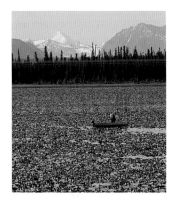

▲ An Athabaskan Native harvests water lilies in a small lake near Kamping Resorts of Alaska.
▶ Vernice Adkins, owner of Kamping Resorts of Alaska, found a new use for the campground's old outhouse.
▶ ▶ A variety of beers, liquors, and wines are sold from the old outhouse during spring and summer.
▶ ▶ ▶ The Kamping Resorts of Alaska gas station and liquor store are popular stops along the Glenn Highway northeast of Anchorage.

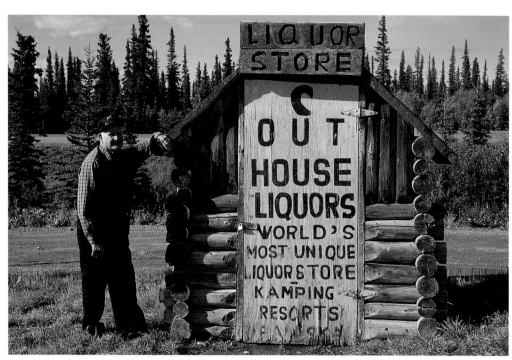

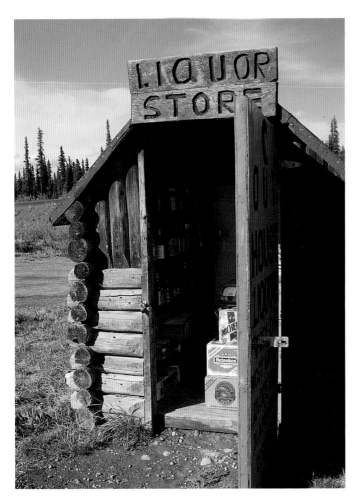

liquor store. Of course. Moved it right out front next to the old gas pump, across the way from the log restaurant and the spot that later would become the Drunken Forest Museum (but that's another story). Put a sign on it to let everyone know what he had done. When I asked if he had ever thought of replacing the outhouse liquor store with a more traditional building, he replied, "Nope. This works out just fine. Serves our purpose."

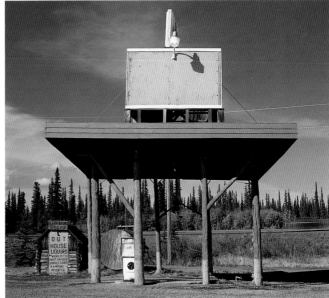

PLASTIC, PORTABLE, AND PLENTIFUL

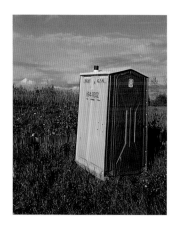

▲ Plastic portable toilets, such as this one in Anchorage's Kincaid Park, dot the landscape of Alaska.
▶ Loaded on a trailer bed, a row of port-a-potties is ready to be moved through the streets of Anchorage.
▶▶ A portable toilet awaits its next visitor in Pop Carr Park in Anchorage.

The construction is of plastic and fiberglass, the decor distinctly sterile, and the personality, well, nonexistent. But a visit to one of the thousands of portable toilets in Alaska is probably the closest thing most tourists and many Alaskans will get to a real outhouse. Called "port-a-potties," "rent-a-cans," or "porta-johns," portable toilets are everywhere in Alaska (except, perhaps, where you need one). Nobody knows for sure how many there are. My phone call to the Federal Environmental Protection Agency was referred to the Western District Office of the State of Alaska Department of Environmental Conservation, which referred me to its Environmental Health Division, which suggested I call a local dealer. A portable toilet dealer in Anchorage responded to my call with suspicion. "I can't tell you how many we have in the field," an employee told me. "Believe it or not, there is a lot of competition in this business. I can only tell you that there are lots of them." ◢ You find portable toilets in all the predictable places: construction sites, campgrounds, roadside rest stops, scenic overlooks, boat ramps, public parks. . . . You can also find them in less likely places. I heard a story about a homesteader, living on the edge of Kachemak Bay near Homer, who looked out her cabin window early one morning and saw a bright green portable toilet floating by on a rising tide. She jumped in her boat, towed the port-a-potty to shore, and set it up behind her cabin, where it sits today.

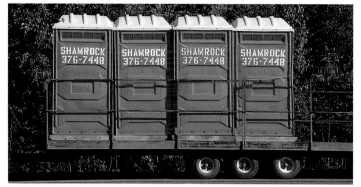

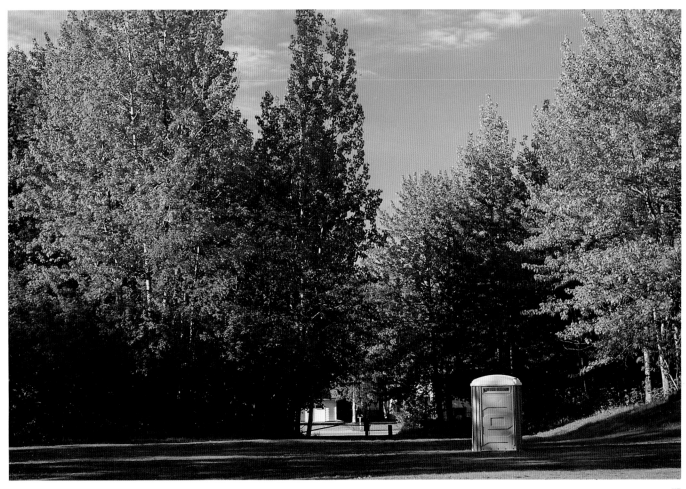

A PLACE TO LOSE TRACK OF TIME

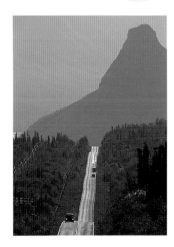

▲ Near the Hernandez home, the Glenn Highway descends in a long straightaway toward a rock called the Lion Head

▶ Michael Hernandez built this outhouse out of logs left over from the construction of the family cabin.

The outhouse Mary and Michael Hernandez use now is a far cry from the one they had in 1988, when they built their log house on the steep flank of Sheep Mountain. Today, their eight-foot-by-eight-foot spruce log outhouse, with hanging flower baskets, a rhubarb garden, and a well-stocked library, is nestled in some trees on a small flat spot overlooking their spruce log house, the Glenn Highway, the Matanuska River, and the snowcapped Chugach Mountains. 🌙 Back in 1988, things were a little different. "The outhouse we started out with was just a little plastic teepee thing," explained Michael, shaking his head. "I hated it. I decided I wanted an outhouse that

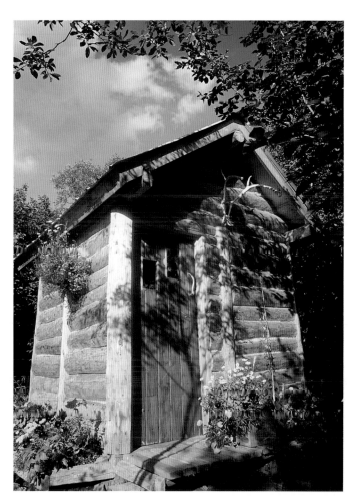

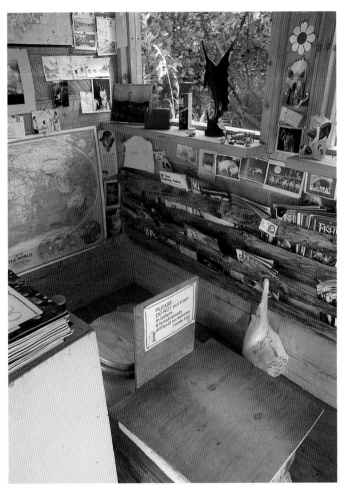

was big enough for me to stand inside of to pull my pants up." 🌙 To make that dream a reality, Michael used a bunch of leftover logs from the construction of the house and went to work on the outhouse in the winter of 1990. When it was finished, Mary decorated it, filling the walls, shelves, and windowsill of the interior with her eclectic collection of knickknacks, posters, photos, maps, and other memorabilia. Her pig collection went on permanent display in the outhouse. "My friend and I got into pigs," Mary explained. "I have no idea why. People have been giving me pig stuff ever since. I can't get away from it." 🌙 "You know, it's amazing how much time people spend out there," Mary said with a laugh. "A friend visited recently, and one morning I bet she spent more than a half hour out there. I was getting ready to go look for her when she came down the hill, all embarrassed and apologetic. Apparently she got to reading some of the stuff on the walls and completely forgot the time."

◄ An array of maps, magazines, posters, and photos—collected by Mary Hernandez—provides outhouse visitors with plenty of distractions.
► The outhouse windowsill displays Mary Hernandez's collection of miniature pigs.

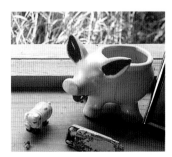

GUARD HOUSE

I no longer remember the first outhouse I ever saw or used in Alaska, but the first one I photographed belonged to the Dixon Creek Mine, a small placer gold mine on the Casadepaga River about seventy-five miles northeast of Nome. Most outhouses built in areas with trees are fairly inconspicuous. But this little outhouse, sitting by itself at the far edge of camp with nothing but miles of tundra beyond, was hard to miss. To me it looked like an old guard house, though I could never figure out if it was there to guard the camp from the wilds of the tundra, or to guard the tundra from the sparse civilization of the camp.

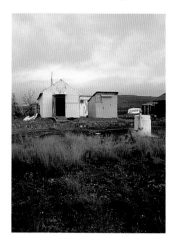

▲ An old washing machine, used by the miners as a washtub, sits in front of a handful of plywood shacks that makes up the Dixon Creek Mine.
▶ A rolling carpet of shrubs, mosses, and lichens surrounds the buildings of the Dixon Creek Mine along the Casadepaga River.
▶ ▶ The lonely outhouse stands at the edge of a vast expanse of barren tundra.

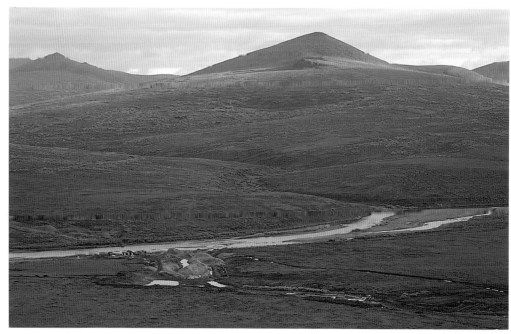

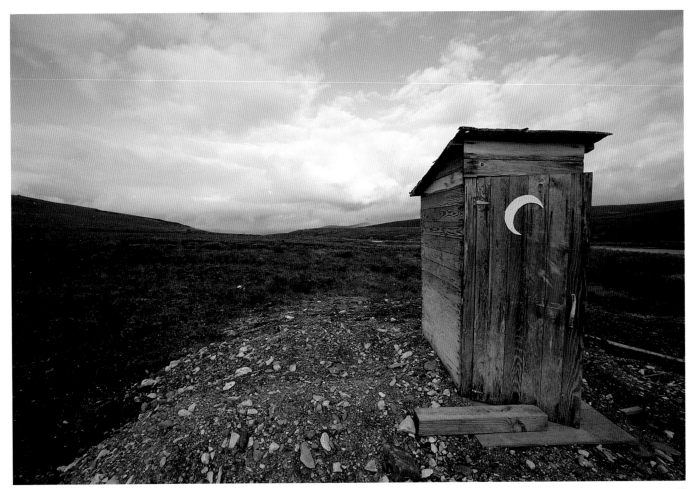

OUTHOUSE SERENADE

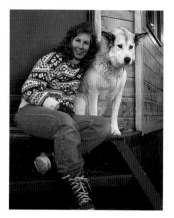

▲ Claire Steffens shares a moment of affection with her dog Nunatak on the steps of her house.
▶ Sunlight filters through a stand of birch trees on a cold afternoon in Anchorage.
▶ ▶ When winter comes, Claire Steffens enjoys the glow from Christmas lights decorating her outhouse.

Claire Steffens has a love-hate relationship with her outhouse. When she moved into the tiny house on a steep hillside overlooking Anchorage in 1981, there was no running water. The little outhouse was all there was, and Claire thought that wasn't much. For one thing, the outhouse didn't have a top half to the Dutch door. "When the Bear Valley winds blew in winter," Claire said, "it was a real adventure. I had to bend over from the waist while sitting in there to hide from the wind." 🌙 The topper came after a couple of years of continuous use, when Claire realized the small hole underneath the outhouse had just about reached capacity. To save what little space she had left, Claire started visiting neighbors more often or held on in the mornings until she got to work. The situation was uncomfortable. She remembers how happy she was when an overnight visitor, a retired Iowa farmer who had grown up with an outhouse, volunteered to clean out the hole. 🌙 In 1985 Claire had indoor plumbing installed. The outhouse has been used mostly for storage since. Over time, her feelings about the outhouse have mellowed. The addition of the Christmas lights was fairly recent. "You know," she said with an embarrassed smile and reddening cheeks, "I may be the only person who has ever sung to her outhouse. I stood there at my back door once, looking at my outhouse, and an old song just came to me. You know the song," she said, and continued in a sweet, slightly off-key voice, "You light up my life. . . ."

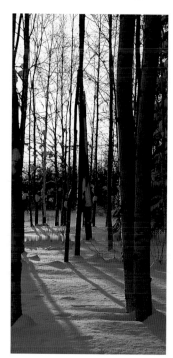

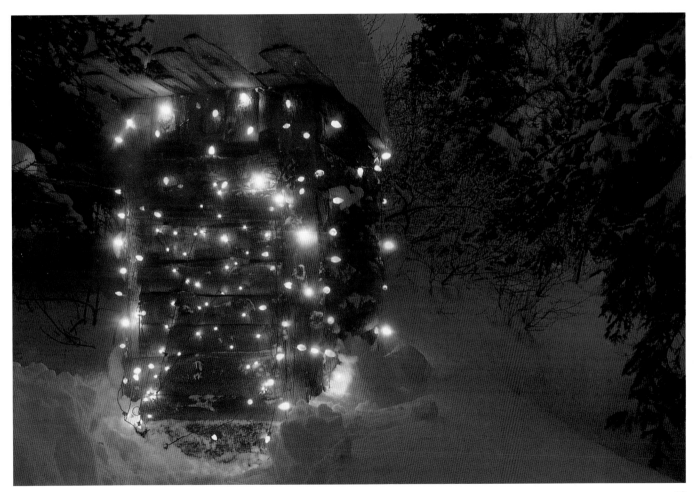

LEST WE FORGET

For more than eighty years, Rika's Roadhouse provided food and lodging to travelers along the Valdez-to-Fairbanks Trail (later the Richardson Highway). The roadhouse was an invaluable oasis in the wilderness, though an oasis without indoor plumbing. So a visit to Rika's included a visit to the roadhouse outhouse. Have historians and archaeologists

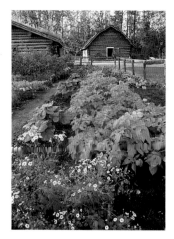

▲ A prosperous vegetable garden offers visitors a look at how Rika's Roadhouse fed its guests in the early 1900s.
▶ Of all the historic buildings that surround the roadhouse, only the outhouse has been ignored and forgotten.

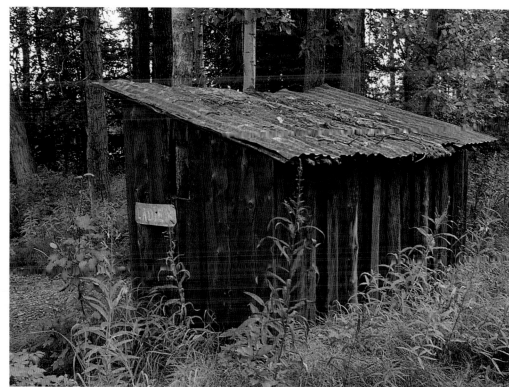

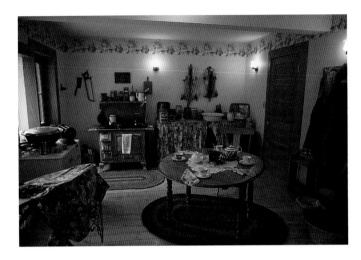

recognized the important role the outhouse played in daily life at the roadhouse? Not hardly. Even with more than a million dollars spent in the last few years studying, stabilizing, and ultimately restoring the roadhouse and other nearby structures, the outhouse has been ignored. ♪ Irene Mead, volunteer park historian and longtime resident of the area, guessed the remaining outhouse was built in the 1930s. "I'm sorry, but we don't really have any information about the outhouse," she confessed. "Nobody's asked." She went on to tell me that of all the pictures she has ever seen of the roadhouse over the years (and there have been many), she remembered only one ever showing an outhouse. "Outhouses were necessary but unmentionable," she said. ♪ Irene went on to tell me about her family's history in the area and about the history of the roadhouse, but on the history of the outhouse she had nothing more to tell. So there the outhouse sits, as much a part of the history of Rika's Roadhouse as any barn or vegetable garden, yet nearly forgotten.

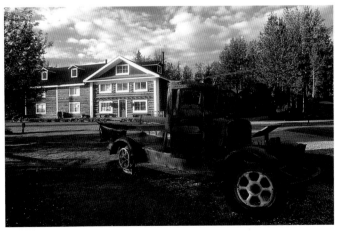

◄ ▲ Historians have restored the interior of the roadhouse to evoke its beginnings as a major stopping point on the wagon road to Fairbanks.
◄ An antique truck is parked outside Rika's Roadhouse, which is part of Big Delta State Historical Park.

COFFEE CAN COMFORTS

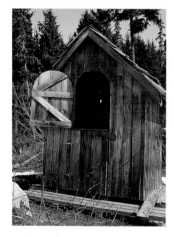

▲ This outhouse, built from rough-hewn boards and handmade shake shingles, sits behind a cabin just off the Haines Highway.
▶ The interior of the outhouse features the finest in color-coordinated accessories.

One of the all-time petty annoyances of using an outside bathroom is damp toilet paper. A roll of toilet paper left lying around in an outhouse will suck up moisture like a sponge. Someone, somewhere, discovered that a two-and-a-half-pound coffee can with a plastic lid was the perfect place to stash a roll of toilet paper to keep it dry. Was this use of a coffee can spontaneously developed by several outhouse owners simultaneously, or was it the work of a single innovator, whose name is now lost? I doubt we will ever know. In either case, this outhouse near the Alaska/Canada border illustrates the classic use of the two-and a-half-pound can. Color coordination between coffee can, toilet seat, and copy of *Time* magazine is a nice touch, but not required.

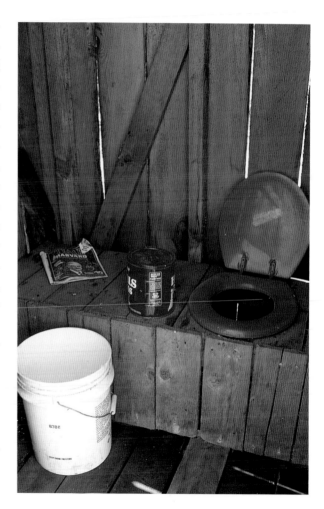

DISAPPEARING ACT

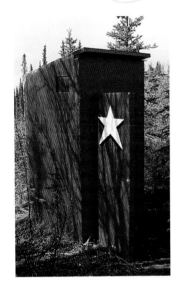

▲ A mysterious outhouse with a fireworks-style paint job: now you see it . . .
▶ . . . now you don't!

I spotted this outhouse while driving back to Anchorage from Valdez. Though partly obscured by trees, the bright red building with a white star stood out against the surrounding green. I pulled off the highway for a closer look. There was no evidence of other buildings. What was an outhouse painted like an actor's dressing room doing here? Not being one to look a gift outhouse in the mouth, I shot a few photos and walked back toward my van. As I reached the edge of the road, I spotted part of a wood platform and a piece of a sign lying in the bush nearby. The sign indicated that a fireworks stand had been located at the pullout, which explained the outhouse's unusual paint job. ◗ A couple of weeks later, I was passing through the area and looked for the outhouse to take a few more photographs. I drove all the way to Glennallen before I realized that I had missed it. On my return trip to Anchorage I looked for the outhouse again, sure that I would find it. Wrong. By the time I realized that I had missed it yet again, I was too tired to turn around. How could I have missed that thing twice? ◗ On my next trip to Glennallen, about three weeks later, I was determined to find that outhouse. I drove so slowly along the highway I was a traffic hazard. I looked at every pullout, flat spot, and gravel pit. Finally, I recognized a dirt pullout next to the highway. It was obvious I hadn't missed the outhouse all those times—someone had up and taken it away! Even then I had to prove to myself that I was indeed in the right spot. I wandered around in the woods looking for the one thing that couldn't have been removed: the outhouse hole. After a few minutes, I found it. ◗ I wonder how many other great outhouses have come and gone the way of that red outhouse with the big white star?

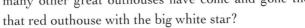

LAST WORD

I was asked recently if I have tried out every outhouse in this book. Honestly, I can't say that I have. It never even occurred to me to do so. For me, the adventure was not using as many outhouses as I could, but rather the challenge of searching for the next really neat outhouse, discovering its secrets, and finding a way to communicate that "something special" through my photographs. And though the book is done, my search for interesting outhouses continues. I am certain there are many more great outhouses out there. Perhaps tomorrow I'll find the best one yet just over the next hill.

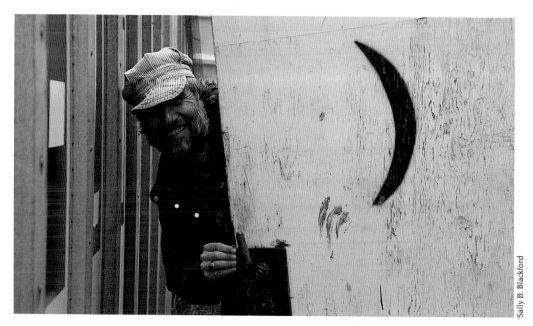

Sally B. Blackford

Photographer and writer Harry M. Walker intimately inspects another outhouse.